MUSICAL INSTRUMENTS

Harps

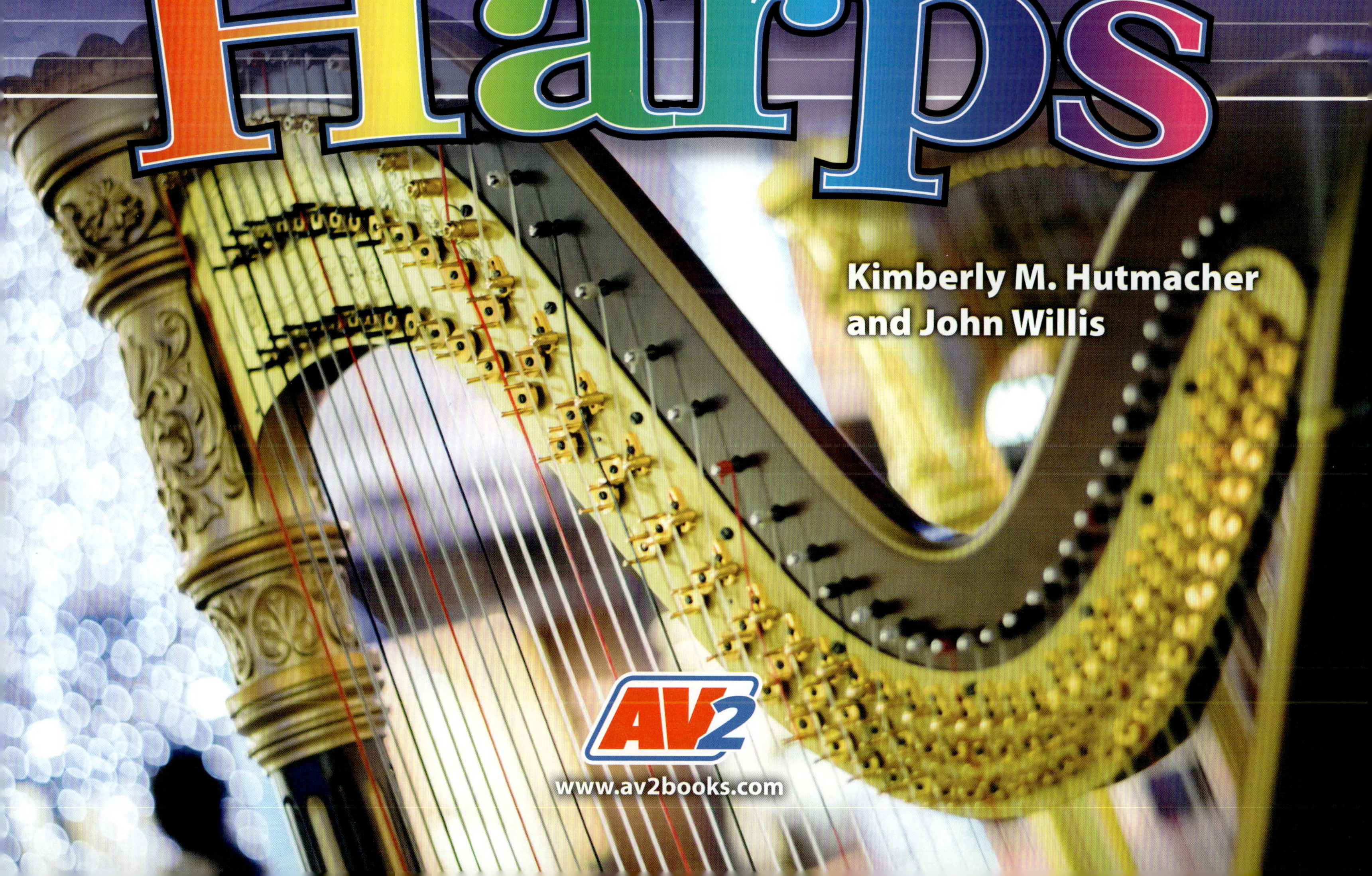

Kimberly M. Hutmacher
and John Willis

AV2
www.av2books.com

AV2

Step 1
Go to **www.av2books.com**

Step 2
Enter this unique code

UPKFR72G4

Step 3
Explore your interactive eBook!

AV2 is optimized for use on any device

Your interactive eBook comes with...

- **Audio** Listen to the entire book read aloud
- **Videos** Watch informative video clips
- **Weblinks** Gain additional information for research
- **Try This!** Complete activities and hands-on experiments
- **Key Words** Study vocabulary, and complete a matching word activity
- **Quizzes** Test your knowledge
- **Slideshows** View images and captions

View new titles and product videos at www.av2books.com

Harps Contents

4

Pluck, *pling*. Pluck, *pling*. The harp makes a pretty sound. It is a fun instrument to play.

A harp has a neck and a body called a sound box. Most harps have pedals and 47 strings.

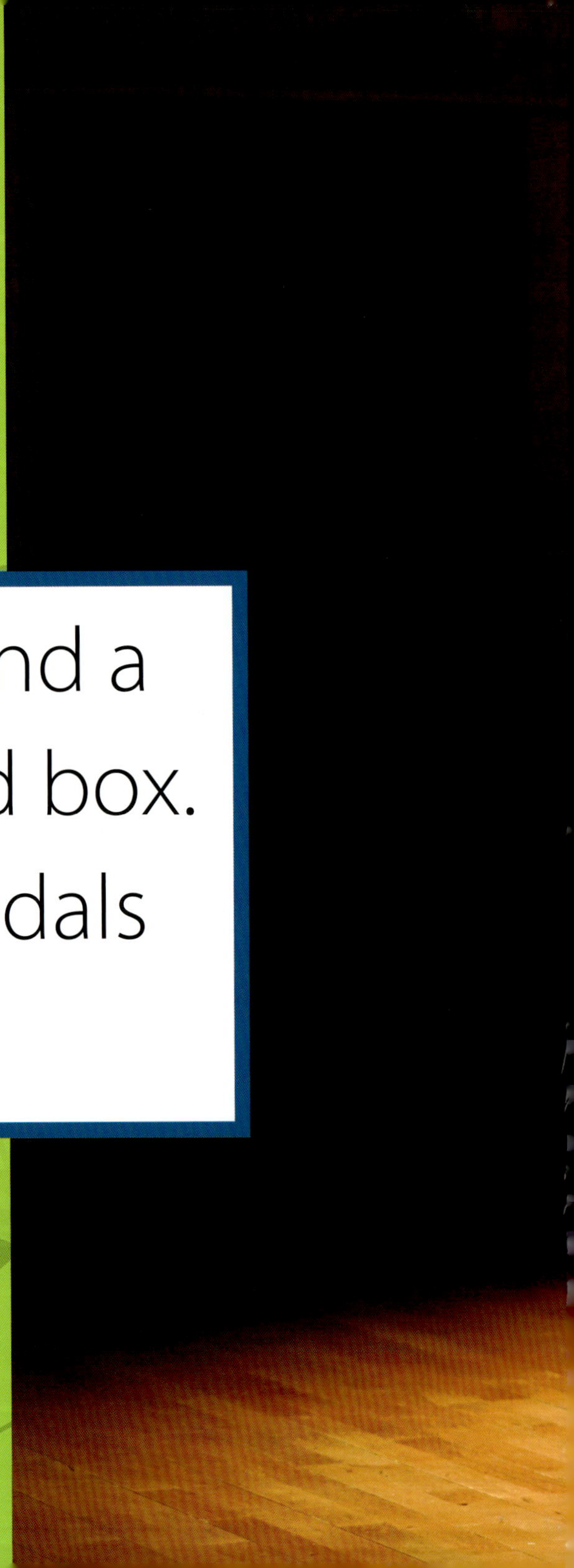

Harp players pluck the strings. They use their thumbs and the first three fingers on each hand.

It takes about 15 minutes to tune a harp's strings.

Each string makes a different sound. Short strings make high sounds. Long strings make low sounds. The pedals help change the sounds.

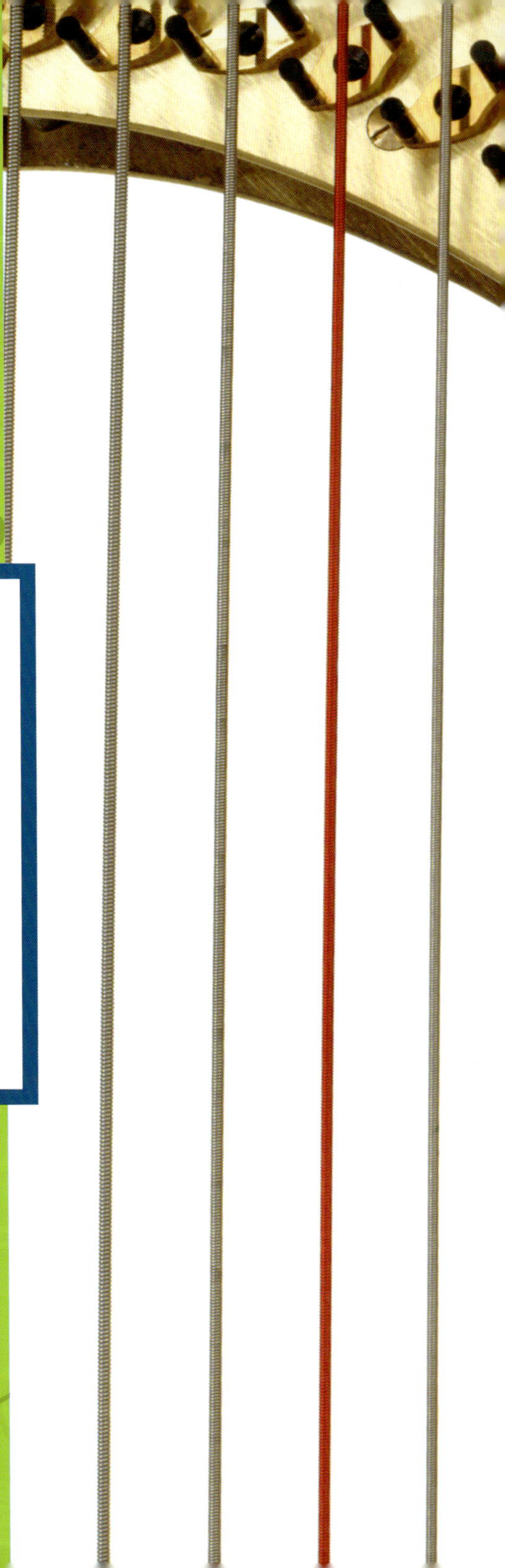

Harp strings are different colors. This helps players find the right string to pluck.

Some harps are carved from just one piece of wood. Other harps have up to 2,000 pieces.

Some harps are more than 6 feet tall. (1.8 meters)

The harp is one of the oldest instruments. Early harps were made from hunting bows.

The first harps were made more than 5,000 years ago.

The harp can be heard in many kinds of music. It is played in classical and rock songs. It is also used for country and folk music.

The harp is mostly played in orchestras. There are one or two harps in an orchestra. They are in the string section.

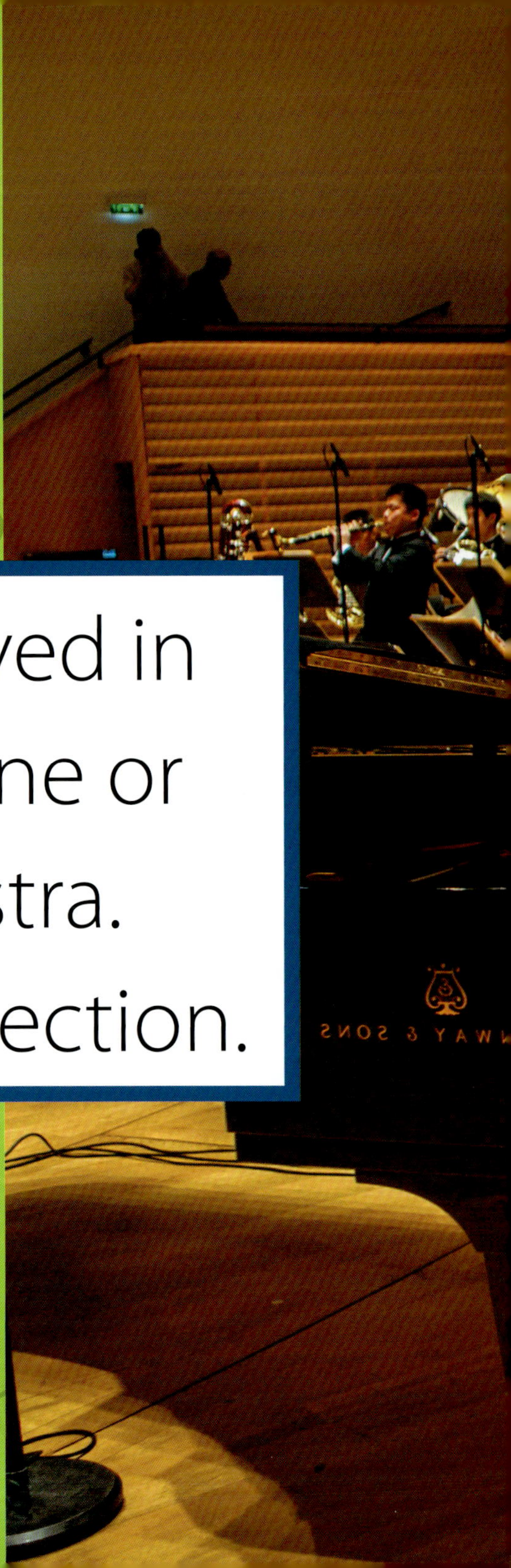

See what you have learned about harps.

Which of these pictures does not show a harp?

KEY WORDS

Research has shown that as much as 65 percent of all written material published in English is made up of 300 words. These 300 words cannot be taught using pictures or learned by sounding them out. They must be recognized by sight. This book contains 57 common sight words to help young readers improve their reading fluency and comprehension. This book also teaches young readers several important content words, such as proper nouns. These words are paired with pictures to aid in learning and improve understanding.

Page	Sight Words First Appearance
5	a, is, it, makes, play, sound, the, to
6	and, has, have, most
9	about, each, first, hand, on, takes, their, they, three, use
10	change, different, help, high, long
12	are, find, right, this
15	feet, from, just, more, of, one, other, some, than, up
16	made, were, years
19	also, be, can, country, for, in, kinds, many, songs
20	an, or, there, two

Page	Content Words First Appearance
5	harp, instrument
6	body, neck, pedals, sound box, strings
9	fingers, minutes, players, thumbs
12	colors
15	piece, wood
16	hunting bows
19	music
20	orchestras, string section

Published by AV2
350 5th Avenue, 59th Floor New York, NY 10118
Website: www.av2books.com

Library of Congress Cataloging-in-Publication Data

Names: Hutmacher, Kimberly, author.
Title: Harps / Kimberly M. Hutmacher and John Willis.
Description: New York : AV2, 2020. | Series: Musical instruments |
Audience: Grades K-1 |
Identifiers: LCCN 2019039619 (print) | LCCN 2019039620 (ebook) | ISBN 9781791116125 (library binding) |
ISBN 9781791116132 (paperback) | ISBN 9781791116149 | ISBN 9781791116156
Subjects: LCSH: Harp--Juvenile literature. | CYAC: Harp.
Classification: LCC ML1005 .H88 2020 (print) | LCC ML1005 (ebook) | DDC 787.9/19--dc23
LC record available at https://lccn.loc.gov/2019039619
LC ebook record available at https://lccn.loc.gov/2019039620

Printed in Guangzhou, China
1 2 3 4 5 6 7 8 9 0 24 23 22 21 20

022020
100919

Project Coordinator: John Willis Designer: Ana María Vidal

The publisher acknowledges Alamy, Getty Images, iStock, and Shutterstock as the primary image suppliers for this title.